Life
Simplify your ~~Practice~~:

Private Judicial Referrals

~ Ohio Revised Code Section 2701.10(B) ~

_____

A unique ADR alternative offering

Final Appealable Orders ....

Judge Michael E. Gilb

Judge Michael E. Gilb

Copyright © Michael E. Gilb
Cover Design by Doug Fortune
No part of this book may be reproduced or transmitted in any
form or by any means, graphic, electronic or mechanical, including
photocopying, recording, taping, or by any information storage
or retrieval system, without the permission
in writing from the author.
Published by
www.iPublishYourBooks.com
Kernersville, NC 27284 USA
Questions/comments -
DougFortune12@gmail.com
Printed in the United States of America

What this book is not ...

This is not a book on the law.

What this book is...

This is a book on procedure.

This book discusses how Private Judicial Referrals:

1. Control your docket....
2. Move your cases quickly...
3. Preserve your rights to appellate review...
4. Let you enjoy your ~~practice~~ – again!
   Life

In the end – Private Judging gives you all of the ADR benefits of a resolution by arbitration – yet, unlike arbitration, Private Judges offer Final Appealable Orders that preserve your right to appellate review.

Judge Michael E. Gilb

Simplify Your Practice: Private Judicial Referrals

CONTENTS

Introduction — vii

Subject Matter Jurisdiction — 1

Statement of the Law & Procedure — 7

Handling Complex Civil Matters — 15

Family Law Matters — 27

Post Script — 37

Statement of the Case

An Introduction

Back in 1982, as I was just then entering law school, a survey conducted by the National Center for State Courts reported that, in the layman's mind, the most serious indictment against our civil justice system was that it took too long and cost too much.[1]

Having practiced law for more than 30 years and having served as a Judge in the General Division of the Warren County Common Pleas Court, I can attest that – in spite of all the advances we have seen (including the increased use of technology in our courtrooms) – in the layman's mind, our civil justice system continues to take too long and cost too much.

An article entitled "Delay in the Courts," reflects that:

> "delay in the courts is bad; ... because it deprives citizens of a basic public service; ... because the lapse of time frequently makes it less likely that justice will be done; ... because it can cause severe hardship on the parties; and ... because it brings to

---

[1] See, Memorandum of T.F. Bridgman and Philip H. Corby to the Illinois Committee to Study Caseflow-Management in the Law Division, Circuit Court, Cook County, Ill., January 8, 1982 – Introduction.

the entire court system a loss of public confidence, respect and pride."[2]

A lawsuit recently filed in Federal District Court in Manhattan depicts a broken justice system in which hundreds of people arrive at the Courthouse each morning only to wait for hours for perfunctory court appearances, often ending up having to return to court repeatedly before having their cases finally resolved.[3]

One of the lead plaintiffs has been quoted: "We see the impact of intractable delays on the lives of our clients every day. They suffer financially and psychologically – losing wages, missing school, scrambling to find child care."[4]

The lawsuit describes people taking time off work, sometimes an entire day, only to find that when they finally do get in front of a judge their appearance lasts just a few minutes before the case is resolved, or worse yet, postponed to another day.[5]

---

[2] See, H. Zeisel, H. Haven and B. Bucholz, "Delay in the Court," Boston, Little Brown & Co., 1959, p. XXIII.

[3] See, Delays in Bronx Courts Violate Defendants' Rights, Lawsuit Says, an article appearing on May 11, 2016, on page A19 of the New York Times; available at http://www.nytimes.com/2016/05/11/nyregion/chronic-bronx-court-delays-deny-defendants-due-process-suit-says.html.

[4] Id.

[5] Id.

It describes the plight of a 40-year-old single mother whose case began in 2012 but wasn't finally resolved until November, 2015 – 1,166 days later.[6] And of a 36-year-old warehouse manager at an appliance company, his case wasn't finally resolved until a bench trial 1,255 days after it was filed. He used overtime as well as vacation days and personal and sick leave to attend many of the court appearances.[7]

While depicting issues of delay in the courts of New York, I suggest that here in Ohio we can all point to similar issues bogging down our justice system here and making life for ourselves and our clients less than ideal.

In the Manhattan lawsuit, the Plaintiffs note that they sought improvements to the justice system that lessen the burdens people coming into contact with the courts are forced to endure.[8]

In Ohio, using Private Judicial Referrals is one of the ways I suggest we can lessen the burdens placed on those individuals seeking to use our civil justice system – things like missing school or work, fighting traffic and congestion, finding and paying for parking [and then – is it parking for 15 minutes or will it be all day ???], securing child care, waiting for a case to be called, all only add to the frustration individual litigants face as they seek to use our

---

[6] Id.
[7] Id.
[8] Id.

civil justice system – and this may be especially so in a crowded courthouse or in many uncontested matters where an appearance in front of a judge may last just a few minutes.

This book explores Ohio's statute on private judging [O.R.C. 2701.10] – adopted in 1984 – and its provision for the parties to *any* civil action or proceeding to refer the matter for adjudication (in its entirety) to a Private Judge.[9]

Private judging is a unique ADR process. ADR systems (arbitration, mediation and private judging) are encouraged because they help to ease judicial bottlenecks, allow for the expeditious resolution of disputes, and open up the judicial process, reducing costs and making justice more affordable to all who seek it.

In the end – Private Judging provides all of the ADR benefits of a resolution by way of arbitration – yet unlike arbitration, it retains all your rights to appellate review.

---

[9] ORC 2701.10(B)(1).

Imagine

Imagine for a moment (both for yourself and your clients): no unnecessary trips to the Courthouse, no fighting traffic or waiting in line, no juggling child care, and no lost time waiting for your case to be called – you control the docket, and you schedule the time and the place for your Final Hearing.

For today's practitioner fully utilizing ORC 2701.10 and its provisions on private judging may make these imaginations possible.

We'll explore in the pages that follow how practitioners might look creatively at O.R.C. 2701.10(B), and at how using a Private Judge could assist them (and their clients) to navigate smoothly and quickly through our civil justice system – again, this would appear especially useful in many uncontested civil matters.

Who knows, employing a private judge may not just lessen a client's burden, it may, in the end, make ~~the practice of law~~ more enjoyable – again!
your Life...

Judge Michael E. Gilb

CHAPTER 1

Subject Matter Jurisdiction

Private Judging

[A unique ADR alternative preserving your right to appellate review]

Private Judging is not a new concept. The statutory authority for private judge proceedings has existed for decades.[10]

The Ohio statute was adopted in 1984 but the concept of private judging dates as far back as 1872. At that time, California had a general reference statute, but it wasn't until the mid-1970's that the idea of using private judges started to blossom.[11]

---

[10] Id. (Ohio's statute was adopted in 1984).
[11] Anne S. Kin, Rent-A-Judges and the Cost of Selling Justice, 44 Duke Law Journal 166-199, at 173 (1994); available at http://scholarship.law.duke.edu/dlj/vol44/iss1/4.

In 1976, three Los Angeles lawyers utilized a private judge to handle a complex commercial case. In 1979, Judge H. Warren Knight, retired from the bench and founded Judicial Arbitration and Mediation Services (JAMS), the first company to offer private judges and soon to become one of the nation's largest providers of alternative dispute resolution services.[12]

The California experience indicates that private judges are most popular in two types of cases: complex civil and family law matters.[13]

In Ohio - used creatively - private judges could be useful in any number of civil matters [consider: uncontested divorces or dissolutions (including post-decree matters); child custody, support and visitation, (including consideration of grandparent rights); paternity; estate and trust matters; guardianships; conservatorships; receiverships; and any other civil matter that requires judicial intervention]. I suggest that private judges may be especially useful in matters which are uncontested but where a Judge's authority is required.

---

[12] Id. at 174; review, Daniel Popeo, Privatizing the Judiciary, first published in the Washington Legal Foundation's Legal Backgrounder series (1988), republished by the Foundation for Economic Education; available at: https://fee.org/articles/privatizing-the-judiciary.
[13] Supra.

Complex Civil Matters

In complex civil matters, private judges are useful because: private judges typically move proceedings quicker than such proceedings would move in the public court system; proceedings are generally more private (and can be held somewhere other than a public courtroom); such proceedings can offer more sensitivity when handling confidential information; and, a private judge is generally more focused (such judge isn't dealing with a crowded docket) and has more specialized knowledge (in public court, judges are randomly assigned to a case and the overall experience of the judge is unknown prior to such random assignment).[14]

Family Law Matters

In family law matters (traditional and non-traditional), a private judge adds privacy to the proceedings – keeping the parties out of a crowded public courtroom (hearings can be held in an attorney's office or another mutually agreeable location); additionally, the proceedings are generally more convenient to the parties (especially useful for uncontested matters). Consider further – a private judge offers practitioners greater flexibility in choosing an appropriate forum (a private judge can generally appear in any of Ohio's 88 counties[15]).

---

[14] Id.
[15] See, ORC 2701.10(A).

Ohio's Experience

Although the Ohio statute has existed since 1984, it has been underutilized – it is a valuable tool for many of today's practitioners.

In Ohio, we already have private judges handling civil and family law matters. The 'pioneer' of private judging in Ohio may be, Private Judge Donald A. Cox. Judge Cox retired from the Gallia County Common Pleas Court bench in 1992. He founded Judicial Alternatives of Ohio, Inc., in 1993, and has been providing mediation, arbitration and private judge services ever since.[16] He offers, what he calls, an innovative and unique "divorce route" that provides private hearings in attorney offices, litigant's homes, public libraries, even nursing homes. His website reports handling cases in more than 30 Ohio counties, conducting more than 100 civil trials and countless mediations and arbitrations.

It is reported that in 2012 private judges heard a substantial portion of the divorces in Franklin County, with Judge Cox handling the majority of those cases.[17] The evidence suggests that the number of private divorce hearings will continue to rise as more couples (traditional

---

[16] See, http://www.privatejudgedonaldcox.com.
[17] See, Many Opt for Private Judges in Franklin County (Couples often use them for dissolution, uncontested divorce), Columbus Dispatch, Feb. 11, 2013; available at: http://www.dispatch.com/content/stories/local/2013/02/11/frequent-use-of-private-judges-in-county-is-rare.html.

and non-traditional) take advantage of the benefits provided by utilizing a private judge: the primary benefit, scheduling – rather than appearing at a crowded Courthouse for hearings or conferences, a private judge can meet the parties at a mutually agreeable time and place[18]; a secondary benefit, privacy in choosing an appropriate forum.

In Ohio, the offering of private judicial services will grow as more Ohio practitioners turn to private judges to handle their civil matters.

Private Judge James L. Kimbler, retired from the Medina County Common Pleas Court bench in January, 2015; he founded NorthCoast ADR Services and through NorthCoast, offers mediation, arbitration and private judging services pursuant to ORC 2701.10.[19] Over the next few years, new companies will be formed to provide Private Judicial Referrals offering arbitration, mediation and private judging services.

The concept of private judging promises to move the practice of law forward in Ohio. Crowded Courthouses, reduced budgets and jammed dockets tend to slow our civil justice system[20]. Constitutional directives

---

[18] Compare: Should You Hire Your Own Private Divorce Judge? Posted January 20, 2015, available at: http://www.divorceattorneysohio.com/2015/01.
[19] See, http://www.northcoastadrservices.com.
[20] Review, Daniel Popeo, Privatizing the Judiciary, first published in the Washington Legal Foundation's Legal Backgrounder series (1988),

mandating preference in criminal cases force more and more civil matters to take a back seat. Fully utilizing ORC 2701.10 and its provisions for private judging permits the parties to *any* civil action or proceeding in any court to have the matter referred (in its entirety) to a Private Judge.[21] The ability to secure a Final Appealable Order from a Private Judge is a unique, and distinguishing, feature of this ADR concept.

---

republished by the Foundation for Economic Education; available at: https://fee.org/articles/privatizing-the-judiciary.

.

CHAPTER 2

Statement of the Law & Procedure

Ohio's Private Judging Statute

[ORC 2701.10]

ORC 2701.10 permits the parties to any civil action or proceeding in any court to have the matter referred for adjudication (in its entirety) to a Private Judge[22].

Once an appropriate referral is made, the Judge before whom the matter is pending in public court "shall order" the referral to the Private Judge.[23] Furthermore, once the Order of referral is put on, the Private Judge has all of the powers, duties and authority of an Active Judge.[24]

Any judgment entered by such Private Judge has

---

[22] See, Note 9.
[23] ORC 2701.10(C).
[24] Id.; see also, note 11, at 170.

the full force and effect of a Final Judgment in a public court.[25]

Any judgment rendered by such Private Judge is fully reviewable on Appeal.[26]

Unlike arbitrators or mediators, Private Judges are officially part of the state court system; their judgments have the same force and effect as judgments of any other state court; and their judgments can be appealed in the state court system.[27]

The Rules on Private Judging

Rule VI of the Supreme Court Rules for the Government of the Judiciary of Ohio[28], sets forth procedural rules for private judging of civil matters referred pursuant to ORC 2701.10(B).

The Rule provides that upon consent of the parties to refer a matter for adjudication to a Private Judge, they shall sign a written agreement that complies with the mandates of the statute (ORC 2701.10(B)(1)(a) to (e))[29].

The statute (ORC 2701.10) anticipates that the parties, and the Private Judge, will enter into a written

---

[25] ORC 2701.10(D); see also, note 11, at 170.
[26] Id.
[27] Id.; see also, note 11, at 166.
[28] See, Supreme Court Rules for the Government of the Judiciary of Ohio, at Rule VI; referred to and cited hereinafter as 'Gov. Jud. R. VI'.
[29] Gov. Jud. R. VI, Sect. 2(A).

agreement – the Referral Agreement[30]. The Referral Agreement is the agreement discussed in Gov. Jud. R. VI, Sect. 2(A) [for illustration purposes a sample agreement is attached to the Rule at Form 3[31]].

The Referral Agreement, at a minimum, must do the following[32]:

- Designate the Private Judge to whom the referral is being made;
- Indicate:
   O (i) whether the entire matter is referred;
   or,
   O (ii) describe the specific issue or question submitted;

- Require the parties to provide all reasonably required facilities, equipment and personnel; and,

- Set forth the Private Judge's compensation.

---

[30] ORC 2701.10(B)(1).
[31] See, Gov. Jud. R. VI, Sect. 5 and Form 3, 'Agreement for Referral or Submission to Private Judge" (the Rule, at Sect. 5, notes that the form is intended for illustration only – substantial compliance with the prescribed form is sufficient. Minor departures that do not negate substantial compliance will not render void forms that are otherwise sufficient, and the forms may be varied when necessary to meet the facts of a particular case); note: Form 3, the Sample Agreement, is reproduced here at the end of this Chapter, it is also available on the Ohio Supreme Court's website and as referenced in the Rule – go to: http://www.sconet.state.oh.us/LegalResources/Rules/government/GOV JUD.pdf.
[32] See, ORC 2701.10(B)(1)(a) – (e).

Once the Referral Agreement is signed, it should be filed with the Clerk of Courts in that Court where the matter is then pending[33]. Best practice would suggest preparation of a Motion and Order for Referral and attaching the Referral Agreement to such Motion[34].

Upon filing the Judge before whom the action is pending – "shall order" – the referral[35].

And once the Order of Referral is put on, the Private Judge has all of the powers, duties and authority of an Active Judge[36].

Any judgment entered by such Private Judge has the full force and effect of a Final Judgment in a public court[37].

Any judgment rendered by such Private Judge is

---

[33] See, Gov. Jud. R. VI, Sect. 2(A).
[34] A sample 'Motion for Referral' is attached immediately following this Chapter; the same is for illustration only.
[35] See, Gov. Jud. R. VI, Sect. 2(B); see also, Sect. 5 and Form 4, 'Order of Referral or Submission to Private Judge" (the Rule, at Sect. 5, notes that the form is intended for illustration only – substantial compliance with the prescribed form is sufficient. Minor departures that do not negate substantial compliance will not render void forms that are otherwise sufficient, and the forms may be varied when necessary to meet the facts of a particular case); note: Form 4, the Sample Order of Referral, is reproduced here at the end of this Chapter, it is also available on the Ohio Supreme Court's website and as referenced in the Rule – go to:
http://www.sconet.state.oh.us/LegalResources/Rules/government/GOVJUD.pdf.
[36] Id.; see also, ORC 2701.10(D).
[37] ORC 2701.10(D).

fully reviewable on Appeal[38].

Unlike arbitrators or mediators, Private Judges are officially part of the state court system; their judgments have the same force and effect as judgments of any other state court; and their judgments can be appealed in the state court system[39].

The Ohio Rules of Civil Procedure and the Ohio Rules of Evidence are fully applicable to actions referred to a Private Judge pursuant to ORC 2701.10[40].

To maintain integrity, the Ohio Supreme Court retains authority over the matter referred as in all other cases[41]; the Private Judge is subject to Ohio's Code of Judicial Conduct[42]; and, the Private Judge is directed to swiftly resolve the matter[43].

Imagine for a moment (both for yourself and your clients): no unnecessary trips to the Courthouse, no fighting traffic or waiting in line, no juggling child care, and no lost time waiting for your case to be called – you control the docket and schedule the time and the place for your Final Hearing.

---

[38] Id.
[39] Id.; see also, Note 11, at 166.
[40] See, Gov. Jud. R. VI, Sect. 3(A).
[41] See, Id., Sect. 4(A).
[42] See, Id., Sect. 4(B).
[43] See, Id., Sect. 3(B), (C) & (D).

Sidebar #1

Cody Flowers Wrongful Death Jury Trial.

Lucas County Common Pleas Court Case No. G-4801-CI-200801532-000.

Prior to becoming a Judge, Michael E. Gilb had been engaged in 2007, in his private legal practice, by Brittany Barger, the mother of Cody Flowers-Barger, to represent Cody in regard to the wrongful death of his father, Cody Flowers.

The decedent, Cody Flowers, was killed in a MVA on 7/3/2007; he was 18.

Prior to Cody Flowers' death, Brittany Barger had become pregnant and at the time of his death, she was carrying Cody Flowers' unborn son, Cody Flowers-Barger.

In August, 2007, Cody Flowers' mother hired her own counsel and attempted to 'settle' the wrongful death action of her son. Legal action was filed on behalf of Cody Flowers-Barger (while he was yet in utero), to prevent Cody Flowers' mother from entering into any settlement regarding Cody Flowers' wrongful death until Cody Flowers-Barger birth in that, if he were born alive, he would be a primary wrongful death beneficiary as the son of the decedent – Cody Flowers-Barger was born alive 2/8/2008.

The decedent, Cody Flowers, had tested positive for alcohol with a .25 BAC and the accident occurred at 4 a.m. on a rural county road in Hardin County, Ohio as he was driving home from a late-night party.

The MVA occurred when a dump truck failed to stop for a stop sign – the driver testified that he 'saw Cody Flowers' vehicle approaching the intersection but thought that there was sufficient time to pass thru and so he did not stop for the stop sign'. His assumptions were inaccurate and Cody Flowers' vehicle impacted the dump truck just behind the driver's side door. Cody Flowers died at the scene.

The Ohio State Hwy Patrol testified that alcohol was not a factor in the accident.

On the 4th day of a 7-day jury trial we were able to resolve the action by way of a settlement. We were able to successfully structure the settlement to provide for Cody Flowers-Barger's future & educational needs.

Judge Michael E. Gilb

CHAPTER 3

Handling Complex Civil Matters

What if there was an Ohio statute that said – in any civil matter – you could:

1. Pick your Judge;

2. Apply Ohio Law, including its Rules of Evidence and Civil Procedure;

3. Secure a "Final Judgment" [like the one you get in a public courtroom];

4. Preserve your rights to appellate review;

5. Obtain effective and efficient case management; all while,

6. Maintaining privacy.

Although all this may sound too good to be true, it's not, it is exactly what Ohio's statute on Private Judging (ORC 2701.10) provides for you.

In the end – Private Judging provides a unique ADR alternative that retains your rights to appellate review; it gives you a Final Appealable Order [like you would secure in a public courtroom].

Ohio's Private Judging Statute

ORC 2701.10 permits the parties to any civil action or proceeding in any court to have the matter referred for adjudication (in its entirety) to a Private Judge[44].

Once an appropriate referral is made, the Judge before whom the matter is pending in public court "shall order" the referral to the Private Judge[45]. Furthermore, once the Order of referral is put on, the Private Judge has all of the powers, duties and authority of an Active Judge[46].

Any judgment entered by such Private Judge has the full force and effect of a Final Judgment in a public court[47].

Any judgment rendered by such Private Judge is fully reviewable on Appeal[48].

Unlike arbitrators or mediators, Private Judges are officially part of the state court system; their judgments have the same force and effect as judgments of any other state court; and their judgments can be appealed in the state court

---

[44] ORC 2701.10(B)(1).
[45] ORC 2701.10(B)(2).
[46] ORC 2701.10(C).
[47] ORC 2701.10(D).
[48] Id.

system[49].

In the end - in any civil matter - you have all the ADR benefits of a resolution by way of arbitration, yet, unlike arbitration, you have a right to appellate review.

Adopted in 1984

Ohio's statute, ORC 2701.10, was adopted in 1984, and in light of the substantial benefits it provides, it is surprising that it is not more widely known and utilized.

It has been suggested that one reason private judging remains under-utilized is because many civil litigants want their case to be decided by a jury[50]. But if using a private judge makes sense, you shouldn't be put off by the insistence of a jury trial; used creatively, litigants should be able to secure the benefits of a private judge without losing the insight they seek in a jury's verdict[51].

The Benefits of a Private Judge

Ohio's private judging statute brings substantial benefits to the parties dealing with Ohio's civil justice system; private judges are useful because:

- private judges typically move proceedings quicker than

---

[49] Id.; see also, Anne S. Kin, Rent-A-Judges and the Cost of Selling Justice, 44 Duke Law Journal 166-199, at 166 (1994); available at: http://scholarship.law.duke.edu/dlj/vol44/iss1/4.
[50] See, Understanding the benefits of a private judge, JAMS Blog, Posted on September 1, 2015, by Hon. Patrick J. Mahoney (Ret.); available at: http://jamsadrblog.com/2015/09/01/understanding-the-benefits-of-a-private-judge-in-california/.
[51] Id.

such proceedings would move in the public court system;

  - proceedings are generally more private (and can be held somewhere other than a public courtroom);

  - proceedings offer more sensitivity for handling confidential information;

  - a private judge is generally more focused (such judge isn't dealing with a crowded docket as in a public courtroom);

  - and a private judge has more specialized knowledge (in public court, judges are randomly assigned to a case and the overall experience of the judge is unknown prior to such random assignment)[52].

Types of Civil Matters

In Ohio - used creatively - private judges could be useful in any number of civil matters – anything from complex civil litigation to private family law matters – it could include civil trials [query: perhaps including advisory juries]; domestic relations matters; paternity; estate and trust matters; guardianships; conservatorships; receiverships; any other civil matter that may require judicial intervention. I suggest that private judges may be especially useful in matters which are uncontested but where a Judge's authority is required.

Complex Civil Litigation

[query: perhaps including advisory juries]

In the practice of law, nothing is as exciting, or

---

[52] Id.

demanding, as a trial by jury; that is, choosing ordinary citizens at random from the community and asking them to make decisions (i.e., render a verdict) that affects people's property, their pocket books, their reputations, and in essence, their very lives[53].

At the start of every jury trial I conducted, I reminded the individuals summoned to jury duty that, when they closed that door behind them in the jury room, they were the government – they were the legal system – and that trial by jury was one of the most valuable rights we possessed.

Concerning an attorney's participation in that process Private Judge James L. Kimbler[54], appropriately reminds us:

> "... Judge your success as a trial lawyer (not upon your won-loss record, but) by the role you have in the process of helping juries and judges render justice in (their) courtrooms. Every time a jury comes back with a verdict it is an affirmation of the American people's ability to govern themselves[55]."

Moving Votes

Decisions made by juries are different from the

---

[53] See. Kimbler, Judge James L., Practice Tips for Trial Attorneys: A Conversation with Judge James L. Kimbler, Sigel Press, 2017, at p. vii.
[54] Judge James L. Kimber served for more than 30 years a judge in Ohio. He conducted over 530 jury trials. He retired from the Medina County Common Pleas Court in January, 2015. He founded NorthCoast ADR Services, and through NorthCoast offers arbitration, mediation and private judging services; see:
http://www.northcoastadrservices.com.
[55] See, Note 53, at p. 109.

decisions you and I make[56]. Our decisions – marriage, career, healthcare – usually only affect us, or the people in our lives. The decisions a jury makes are different; they are different because the decisions a jury makes doesn't affect the individual jurors directly, rather, their decisions only affect the parties to the litigation[57].

Having run a number of political campaigns (as a State Representative, City Council Member and as a Judge), I can attest (even as Private Judge Kimbler suggests[58]) that lawyers trying cases and politicians face similar dilemmas: They both are required to move votes; that is, to persuade a group – either jurors or voters – to make a decision that doesn't affect them directly[59]. The voters don't assume the office, nor do jurors become obligated on any judgment rendered[60].

Political operatives know that they are not going to change social or cultural values during the limited time they have to run a political campaign. They craft a campaign message that considers the cultural values already existing in the minds of the voters.

Likewise, during the limited time an attorney has to try a case, they aren't going to change the values and beliefs individual jurors bring with them into the jury box – counsel must impart a theme for their case that considers those values and yet moves jurors to find in favor of their client[61].

---

[56] See, Id., at p. vii.
[57] Id.
[58] See, Note 53.
[59] See also, Id., at p. 12.
[60] See, Id.
[61] See, Id., at 16.

Simplify Your Practice: Private Judicial Referrals

Understanding all this, if using a Private Judge makes sense in a particular civil matter, don't be put off by the insistence of a jury trial; used creatively, litigants should be able to secure the benefits of a private judge without losing the insight they seek in a jury's verdict[62]; additionally, you may have a civil matter that doesn't require a jury, certainly then, the use of a private judge gives you all the benefits noted above.

Private Judge – *Consulting*

Even though you may decide to stick it out in public court, you should consider consulting with a private judge on issues that affect your case.

Certainly a Private Judge has been in the trenches; he or she has seen the issues you wrestle with in your particular case.

A Private Judge has experience handling discovery, motions, evidence and understanding juries. A Private Judge knows that – much like the voters in a political campaign – although juries make mistakes, they generally get it right[63]; that a trial tells a story, and that the story being told in your case has to resonate with a jury and the values and beliefs of the individual jurors.

Consulting with a Private Judge – on discovery, evidentiary issues, motions, or even preparation for trial – are all things that can benefit your case even if you have decided to

---

[62] See, Note 50.
[63] See, Note 53, p. viii.

stay inside a public courtroom[64].

Other Civil Matters

Private Judges could be useful in any number of civil matters.

I've devoted the entire next chapter to Family Law Matters[65] – divorce (contested or uncontested), dissolution, collaboration (including post-decree matters); child custody, support and visitation, (including consideration of grandparent rights) – there are many other civil matters (some of which even your author may not have yet considered) that could benefit from using a Private Judge; things like: estate and trust matters; guardianships; conservatorships; receiverships; any other civil matter that may require judicial intervention. I suggest that Private Judges may be especially useful in matters which are uncontested but where a Judge's authority is required.

Meeting Client Goals

People often complain about being summoned for jury duty (even though in the end they generally find the experience of serving on a jury to be rewarding). I could write a book on the number of letters I received during the time I served as Judge in the General Division of the Warren County Common Pleas from individuals summoned to jury duty and detailing the 'hardships' such service would impose upon them. Until someone had served on a jury they would write describing how they couldn't perform jury duty because they would miss school

---

[64] See also, Note 53, and the practical advice provided on trial preparation.
[65] See, Chapter 4.

or work, lose income, would struggle with child care issues, transportation and many other inconveniences caused by the call to serve.

In much the same way, clients have similar concerns as they pursue justice and wrestle with requirements that they appear in front of a judge – this is especially so when appearing in a crowded courthouse or in many uncontested matters that require only a few minutes in front of a judge.

If we can lessen these burdens – things like missing school or work, losing income, fighting traffic and congestion, finding and paying for parking [and then – is it parking for 15 minutes or will it be all day ???], securing child care, waiting for a case to be called (and again, especially so in uncontested matters) – then we should seek to do so.

Ohio's statute on private judging [O.R.C. 2701.10] – adopted in 1984 – and its provision for the parties to any civil action or proceeding to refer the matter for adjudication (in its entirety) to a Private Judge – is something we should consider.

Imagine for a moment (both for yourself and your clients): no unnecessary trips to the Courthouse, no fighting traffic or waiting in line, no juggling child care, and no lost time waiting for your case to be called – you control the docket and schedule the time and the place for your Final Hearing.

For today's practitioner fully utilizing ORC 2701.10 and its provisions on private judging may make these imaginations possible. Who knows, employing a private judge may not just lessen a client's burden, it may, in the end, make the practice of law more enjoyable – again!

Sidebar #2

Justin P. Whitman v. Jeffrey J. Whitman.

Hancock County Probate Court Case No. 20074002A.

Prior to becoming a Judge, Michael E. Gilb had been engaged in 2006, in his private legal practice, by Justin Whitman, to pursue an accounting for and recovery of funds which Justin's father, an attorney, Jeffrey Whitman, held in various Uniform Gift to Minor Accounts since 1994 and which were not delivered to Justin following his reaching age 21 in January, 2005.

In 2006, a written request for an accounting of the funds was made.

In 2007, a Petition for an Accounting was filed in Probate Court. Following a trial in July, 2008, an Order that Jeffery Whitman provide an accounting was put on.

Upon failure to abide by that Court's Order a contempt action was filed and following a number of hearings and an independent accounting, in April, 2010, the Court Sentenced Jeffrey Whitman in contempt for failure to account. [The Court ordered the immediate delivery of $215,000 to Justin and additionally issued a 3-day jail sentence on the contempt].

Appeals ensued by Jeffrey Whitman, and in 2012 the Court of Appeals issued a unanimous decision upholding the sentence imposed by the Trial Court. The Appellate Court's Decision was published at:

Justin Whitman vs. Jeffrey Whitman, 2012-Ohio-405 (3rd Dist., 2012).

Simplify Your Practice: Private Judicial Referrals

In 2012, an action for damages was filed against Jeffrey Whitman [Hancock County Common Pleas Court, Case No. 2012CV0300]; that action resolved by way of a confidential settlement in 2016.

CHAPTER 4

Family Law Matters

[traditional & non-traditional]

Hiring a "Private Judge" in a family law matter may sound like something only a Donald Trump could do[66], but in Ohio using a Private Judge[67] provides a unique opportunity for today's family law practitioner to meet a client's most important goals.

Meeting Client Goals

Goals like reducing stress and maintaining privacy:

- Privacy both in terms of the place of filing (a private judge can appear in any of Ohio's 88 Counties) and the

---

[66] See, "Should you hire your own private judge? (You can't buy your verdict but you can pay for a speedier trial)," by Geoff Williams, U.S. News Money Magazine, July 18, 2013; available at: http://money.usnews.com/money/personal-finance/articles/2013/07/18/should-you-hire-your-own-private-judge.

[67] ORC 2701.10(B).

place of hearing (private judge proceedings can be held in an attorney's office, a litigant's homes, or any agreeable location).

- Stress in terms of things like taking time off school or work, losing income, fighting traffic and congestion, finding and paying for parking [and then, is it parking for 15 minutes or will it be all day ???], securing child care, and waiting for their case to be called.

All these things only add to the uneasiness clients associate with using Ohio's civil justice system – things they find frustrating, and then especially so once they discover that all they have is an uncontested matter, resolved with just a few minutes in front of a Judge.

Today's client is fast-paced and goal oriented. They are interested in keeping things moving, doing things online (ex.: paying bills and shopping) and employing technology to assist them in completing everyday tasks. For them, to the extent a Private Judicial Referral can move them quickly and smoothly through the civil justice system [bringing them the same outcome (i.e., an Appealable, Final Judgment)] – is something they would welcome and embrace.

Remember, clients are concerned with privacy - and this is especially true in terms of the family law matters they wrestle through. Ending a marriage is difficult and having the ability to maintain privacy in selecting an appropriate court for filing and being able to select the time and place for their Final Hearing (and again, especially in uncontested matters – divorce or dissolution) are all important considerations.

Simplify Your Practice: Private Judicial Referrals

In terms of using Private Judicial Referrals keep in mind:

You aren't 'buying' a Judge

First and foremost, clients should understand that they are not 'buying' a judge. Technically, arrangements are made in accordance with the law and procedure in Ohio[68] to have a case referred for adjudication (entirely or in such part as the parties may choose) to a Private Judge[69].

Ohio Law and the Ohio Supreme Court have established guidelines and rules regarding Private Judging[70].

Notwithstanding, it's important to note that once the Order of referral is put on, the Private Judge has all of the powers, duties and authority of an Active Judge[71]. Any judgment entered by such Private Judge has the full force and effect of a Final Judgment in a public court[72]. Any judgment rendered by such Private Judge is fully reviewable on Appeal[73].

In the end, judgments will be made [a Final Judgment will be put on] – either in a public courtroom or by a Private Judge (judgments similar in kind and style) and even though both parties often split the costs of a Private Judge's compensation, one or the other of those parties may not like the final judgments rendered. The good news here: unlike arbitrators or mediators, Private Judges are officially part of the state court system; their judgments have the same force and

---

[68] See, Infra., Chapter 2.
[69] ORC 2701.10(B)(1).
[70] See, Note 68.
[71] ORC 2701.10(B); see also, Note 11, at 170.
[72] ORC 2701.10(D); see also, Note 11, at 170.
[73] Id.

effect as judgments of any other state court; and their judgments can be appealed in the state court system[74]. [You get all of the ADR benefits without losing your right to appellate review].

Advantages and Disadvantages of using a Private Judge

As with most things in life, there are advantages and disadvantages to using a Private Judge in a family law matter.

The Advantages

First, a Private Judge provides an important alternative. State funding dilemmas continue to plague our courts. When a court's budget gets cut it's no surprise that it affects that court's efficiency and ability to handle cases in a timely manner. Using Private Judicial Referrals provide an alternative. As budgets continue to decline there will be more of a demand for Private Judges[75].

Second, you can get your case tried more quickly – in days versus months – and certainly much quicker than you get in the public court system. Once a referral is made and an Order of Referral is put on the parties and the Private Judge move quickly to agree on a time and place for the Final Hearing. Unlike a public court where the parties are told to show up to a crowded courthouse on a certain date, the parties have more control in terms of setting a time and place for their hearing that makes sense to them. The process of divorce or dissolution will move much quicker (certainly quicker than in a public court) because a Private Judge is only interested in the case before him or her

---

[74] Id.; see also, Note 11, at 166.
[75] See, Note 66.

and, unlike their public court colleague, a Private Judge doesn't have to deal with thousands of cases.

Third, you can choose your judge - within reason, as the other party in the dispute also has to approve the judge, as does the court. Regardless, this is a powerful incentive for people considering a Private Judge[76]. In many family law matters usually only one attorney is involved and that attorney can only represent one spouse, the non-represented spouse usually waives counsel – such party can also thereafter agree to the use of a Private Judge to conduct the Final Hearing and render a Final Judgment. In a public court, judges are assigned randomly – but with a Private Judge you find someone both parties can agree on.

Fourth, a Private Judge has more time to dedicate to just your case. This is different from hearing the case quickly, this deals with how much time a Private Judge has for the specific facts of your case as well as the law that may apply to it. A judge in a public court has to juggle many cases. Imagine if there are multiple divorce and dissolution cases on the docket and one of those is yours. Then imagine that you have a Private Judge dedicated solely to your case for an entire morning or a full day. Under which of these scenarios do you believe your case will get the most attention? A Private Judge may simply have more time because he or she has less cases to handle.

Fifth, the privacy factor. In addition to privacy as to the place of filing and the place of hearing, parties often have information that needs to be shared with each other and the judge but which they don't want out in the public domain.

---

[76] See, Note 66.

Hearings conducted by Private Judges, although still considered public hearings, are usually held privately; using a Private Judge allows you stay off the public radar. In a public courthouse anyone can just walk in to the courtroom – that generally doesn't happen when you're meeting with a Private Judge at your attorney's office or another mutually agreed location[77].

The Disadvantages

First, cost. Perhaps the biggest disadvantage to using a Private Judge may be the cost. Costs vary depending on the Private Judge, who typically sets his or her own fees, and the complexity of the case[78]. Typically, a Private Judge proceeding can cost between $425 and $795 dollars per hour, with the parties often splitting that expense.

Second, getting the right Judge. Do your homework before selecting a Private Judge. Basic information may be available online and information may be available from practicing attorneys in the community. However, Private Judging is a relatively new practice and many lawyers may not be familiar with the idea[79].

Third, consider your case. Not all cases are right for private judging. In some cases - for instance a contentious divorce - staying in a public courtroom may be best for everyone. Where one of the parties is belligerent or prone to violence a Private Judge may not be the right choice. There are times when the decorum, security and formality of a public

---

[77] See, Note 66.
[78] Id.
[79] Id.

courtroom are not replaceable[80].

Maintain perspective

From a client's perspective, using Private Judicial Referrals will make sense if it helps meet their goal of securing a Final Judgment – especially so, if that result can be achieved in a quicker, with more focus, greater privacy and less frustration.

A Private Judge issues a Final Judgment just like the Judgment a public court issues – and, in the end, that's what matters most to our clients. [It provides a unique ADR alternative that allows you to secure a Final Appealable Order].

Using a Private Judge in a family law matter may not just work to lessen a client's burden, it may make the practice of law enjoyable – again!

---

[80] Id.

Sidebar #3

Janessa L. Marksberry vs. The Estate of Gerald L. Marksberry,

Hamilton County Probate Court Case No. 2011003906.

Prior to becoming a Judge, Michael E. Gilb had been engaged, in his private legal practice, in 2011, to prosecute a Will Contest action on behalf of, Janessa Marksberry, the adopted daughter of the decedent, Gerald L. Marksberry.

Shortly after the adoption of Janessa, the decedent, Gerald Marksberry, suffered a severe and debilitating stroke; he was bedridden and in need of 24 hour care.

The decedent, Gerald Marksberry and Janessa's mother, separated following the stroke and Gerald re-located to Cincinnati to reside with his parents.

The decedent, Gerald Marksberry, essentially had limited funds for most of his life; notwithstanding, he had executed a Will leaving 1/4th of his estate to his adopted daughter, Janessa Marksberry; the balance he had bequeathed to his natural daughter, Jamie Marksberry.

In 2010, and shortly before Gerald Marksberry's death in 2011, both of Mr. Marksberry's parents passed away leaving $1.2 Million Dollars of GE Stock to Gerald Marksberry.

In January, 2011, Gerald's first ex-wife and his natural daughter, Jamie Marksberry, assumed care of him. They secured new counsel to prepare a new Will leaving his entire estate to his natural daughter, Jamie Marksberry.

Gerald executed this new Will on February 15, 2011, he died 6 days later on February 22, 2011.

Following completion of discovery, and after the case was set for a jury trial, a successful settlement was reached resolving the matter in favor of Janessa.

Judge Michael E. Gilb

CHAPTER 5

Post-Script

The Closing Argument

The ADR benefits of mediation (pursuant to ORC Chapter 2710) and arbitration (pursuant to ORC Chapter 2711) are widely known and embraced. These ADR systems are embraced and encouraged because they help to ease judicial bottlenecks, allow for the expeditious resolution of disputes, and open up the judicial process, reducing costs and making justice more affordable to all who seek it.

Private judging is another ADR process that the Ohio legislature provided through a statute [ORC 2701.10(B)] adopted more than 30 years ago, in 1984. It is surprising that Private Judging is not more widely known and utilized.

Private Judging is a unique ADR process, that, in the end, provides all of the ADR benefits of a resolution by way of arbitration – yet unlike arbitration, you secure a Final

Appealable Order and you to retain all of your rights to appellate review in the state court system.

Imagine

Imagine for a moment: no unnecessary trips to the Courthouse, no fighting traffic or waiting in line, no juggling child care, and no lost time waiting for your case to be called – you control the docket and schedule the time and the place for a Final Hearing.

For today's practitioner fully utilizing ORC 2701.10 and its provisions on private judging make these imaginations possible.

Who knows, employing a private judge may not just lessen a client's burden, it may, in the end, make the practice of law more enjoyable – again!

ABOUT THE AUTHOR

Judge Michael E. Gilb (Former Judge, Warren County Common Pleas Court) was born in Southwest Ohio. He lived in Greenhills (a Cincinnati suburb) and he is the third oldest of seven children.

Judge Gilb started out studying towards the priesthood. During his first few years of high school he attended St. Francis Seminary in Mt. Healthy, Ohio. He left the seminary after meeting, Michelle; they married in 1981 and remain married today. They have 3 children, Michael Joshua, Alissa and Ashley, and 3 grandchildren.

After leaving the seminary, Judge Gilb graduated from Greenhills High School. He attended the University of Cincinnati where he earned a Bachelor's Degree in law enforcement. He considered working for the Cincinnati Police Department but was encouraged to go to law school.

Judge Gilb attended law school at Ohio Northern University and he graduated near the top of his law school class. Judge Gilb received his license to practice law from the Ohio Supreme Court in 1985 and practiced law for more than 30 years before he became a Judge in the Warren County Common Pleas Court.

Prior to becoming Judge, he had been elected to serve as a State Representative and he served three terms (six years) at the Statehouse in Columbus. After leaving the Statehouse he moved his family to Warren County.

Judge Gilb served on Mason City Council and as a Mediator and Visiting Magistrate in Mason Municipal Court. Following the retirement of Judge James L. Flannery, he became a Judge in the Warren County Common Pleas Court.

Upon completion of his term of service on the Common Pleas Bench, Judge Gilb (former) became the Executive Director of Private Judicial Referrals, Ltd. – a unique ADR Company that offers arbitration, mediation and private judge services.

You can learn more about this unique ADR concept by contacting Judge Gilb and Private Judicial Referrals, Ltd., at: 513-335-2287, or at: michaelgilb@yahoo.com.